BOILING POINT

Understanding Earth's Rising Temperatures

by Golriz Golkar

Consultant:
Sanya Carley, PhD
Kleinman Center for Energy Policy
University of Pennsylvania
Philadelphia, Pennsylvania

CAPSTONE PRESS
a capstone imprint

Published by Capstone Press, an imprint of Capstone
1710 Roe Crest Drive, North Mankato, Minnesota 56003
capstonepub.com

Copyright © 2025 by Capstone. All rights reserved. No part of this publication may be reproduced in whole or in part, or stored in a retrieval system, or transmitted in any form or by any means, electronic, mechanical, photocopying, recording, or otherwise, without written permission of the publisher.

Library of Congress Cataloging-in-Publication Data is available
on the Library of Congress website.

ISBN: 9781669089230 (hardcover)
ISBN: 9781669089247 (paperback)
ISBN: 9781669089254 (ebook PDF)

Summary: Record-high temperatures that are broken and reset three times in one week. Endless heat waves that happen year-round. Heat so intense it spawns raging wildfires. Our planet is getting hotter and hotter. What is behind Earth's rising temperatures, what toll are they taking on living things, and what can be done about them? Packed with information, dynamic photos, and hands-on activities, this book reveals why Earth's temperatures are rising, how governments and industries are working to combat the problem, and what each one of us can do to help keep our planet from reaching its boiling point.

Editorial Credits
Editor: Christopher Harbo; Designer: Tracy Davies; Media Researcher: Svetlana Zhurkin; Production Specialist: Katy LaVigne

Image Credits
Getty Images: AFP/Cristina Quicler, 14, Alistair Berg, 28, Justin Sullivan, 21, Lisa Maree Williams, 20, Mario Tama, 4; NASA Earth Observatory: 5; Newscom: Sipa USA/SOPA Images/ Shawn Goldberg, 25; Shutterstock: AlenKadr, 15 (glass jar and plastic wrap), amdadphoto, 13, anatoliy_gleb, 26, AngieYeoh, 15 (vinegar and soda), Anthony Ricci, 17, Apisit Suwannaka (fire and ice), cover and throughout, ArielMartin (smoke), cover and throughout, Clara Bastian, 9, Designua, 10, 12, Dreamframer, 6, jkcDesign (thermometer), cover and throughout, Nandalal Sarkar, 7, Npeter (Earth), cover and throughout, Olga Popova, 15 (thermometer), PintoArt, 27, rblfmr, 23, Scharfsinn, 24, stockphotofan1, 29, testing, 8, Tony Campbell, 11, Vasilis Ververidis, 18, warat42 (clouds), cover and throughout, Yellow Cat, 15 (rubber bands), zhengzaishuru (water droplets), cover and throughout

Any additional websites and resources referenced in this book are not maintained, authorized, or sponsored by Capstone. All product and company names are trademarks™ or registered® trademarks of their respective holders.

Printed and bound in China. 6096

TABLE OF CONTENTS

A SIZZLING SUMMER

The summer of 2023 was the hottest recorded on Earth. On July 3, National Aeronautics and Space Administration (NASA) scientists measured the hottest day ever on the planet. Just three days later, that record was broken. Throughout the summer, heat waves swept through North America, Europe, and Asia. Wildfires raged in Greece and Canada. At the same time, heavy rains fell in parts of Europe and Asia. While some people suffered from heat, others were stuck in floods. By the year's end, scientists declared 2023 the hottest year on Earth in the last 125,000 years.

Since the 1980s, each decade has been warmer than the one before. **Climate change** is raising Earth's temperature and causing weather patterns to change. Sometimes these weather patterns cause extreme weather and natural disasters. Storms, wildfires, and floods are some examples. Tornadoes, hurricanes, and **droughts** are also extreme weather. Rising temperatures are making life more challenging for all living things, but there is still hope for keeping Earth from reaching a boiling point.

Phoenix, Arizona, experienced its worst heat wave in 2023 with temperatures in July reaching at least 110 degrees Fahrenheit (43 degrees Celsius) for 31 days in a row.

Summer 2023 Heat Map

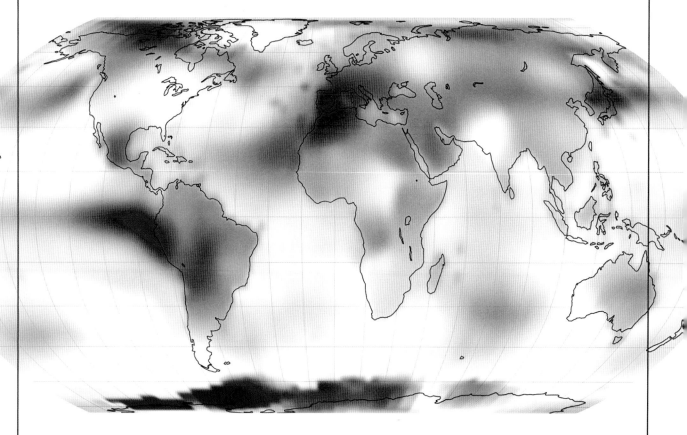

Heat maps use colors to show the planet's temperatures in different parts of the world. NASA's map for the summer of 2023 showed the warmest June, July, and August ever recorded. The orange and red colors show areas that were warmer than long-term average temperatures recorded from 1951 to 1980. During the summer of 2023, heat waves caused extreme temperatures that fueled droughts and wildfires.

FACT —————————

NASA collects weather data around the globe. Weather stations measure land surface air temperatures. Ships collect sea surface temperatures. Satellites in space measure changes in sea ice. NASA studies the data to calculate changes in global temperatures over time.

CHAPTER 1

WHY IS EARTH GETTING HOTTER?

Earth is getting hotter at a rapid rate. But what's behind the rising temperatures?

Over the past century, human activities have changed. Many animals and crops are raised on larger farms than before. Forests are cut down to make room for roads and buildings. Cars have become a common form of transportation. Popular products, from computers and smartphones to clothing and toys, are made every day in factories. But these human activities—and many others—are driving climate change. They are making the planet hotter.

Vast farmlands on California's Pacific coast

Human-Driven Climate Change

When it comes to human-driven climate change, **greenhouse gases** are at the heart of the problem. These gases include carbon dioxide, methane, and nitrous oxide. Small amounts of these gases are found naturally in the **atmosphere**. They create a greenhouse effect that traps heat from the sun. This heat makes the planet warm enough for living things to survive.

But certain human activities release large amounts of greenhouse gases. These gases are especially harmful. They trap even more heat than normal. They are a major reason why Earth is getting hot faster.

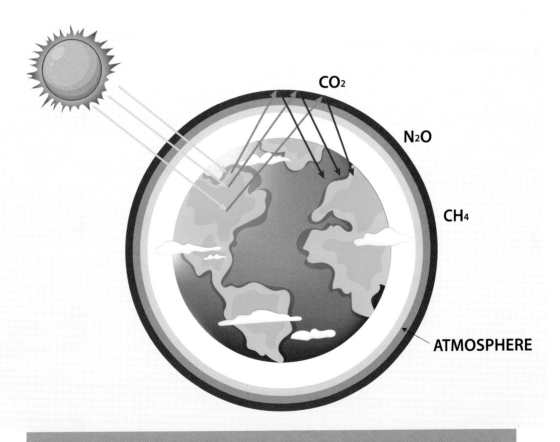

The greenhouse effect happens when gases in Earth's atmosphere trap heat from the sun. Carbon dioxide (CO_2), nitrous oxide (N_2O), and methane (CH_4) are three of the main greenhouse gases causing the planet to warm.

Major Causes of Greenhouse Gases

Many human activities release greenhouse gases. Factories release large amounts of carbon dioxide when they make clothes, building materials, and other products. Most cars, airplanes, trains, and ships also release greenhouse gases. They often burn gasoline and other fuels. Even our homes are driving up Earth's temperature. The electricity to heat and cool them is often created by burning coal.

Livestock farming and landfills also release large amounts of greenhouse gases. Cows release methane into the air when they burp and pass gas. Landfills give off methane as plant and animal matter slowly **decomposes**.

But creating extra greenhouse gases is just part of the problem. People also increase the levels of these gases in the atmosphere through **deforestation**. Forests absorb huge amounts of carbon dioxide from the atmosphere. Plants and trees use this gas and produce the oxygen people and animals need to breathe. When forests are cleared for agriculture or construction, more carbon dioxide remains in the atmosphere.

Congested traffic in Beijing, China

Livestock Farming and Methane Emissions

Livestock farming is an important food source. But cattle, as well as sheep and goats, release large amounts of methane into the atmosphere. These animals have a stomach part called a rumen. **Bacteria** in the rumen are involved in digestion. As the bacteria help digest food, methane is released as a by-product. Farmers are working to reduce methane **emissions** by changing how and what they feed their livestock. Certain foods that are higher in **carbohydrates** and fats use different rumen bacteria for digestion. These bacteria produce less methane. Grinding food and forming food into pellets also helps these animals digest better, reducing their gas emissions.

Shifting Climate Patterns

Changes in Earth's climate patterns also have big impacts on global temperatures. Normally, east winds blow west along the **equator**. Warm water in the Pacific Ocean moves west from South America toward Asia. Cold water rises from the ocean's depths to replace the warm water.

But every two to seven years, a climate pattern called El Niño happens. This climate pattern begins in spring and lasts nine to 12 months. During El Niño, east winds weaken. Warm water moves east toward the west coast of North and South America. As ocean waters warm, more rain clouds form. Parts of North, Central, and South America get more rain than usual. Many areas flood.

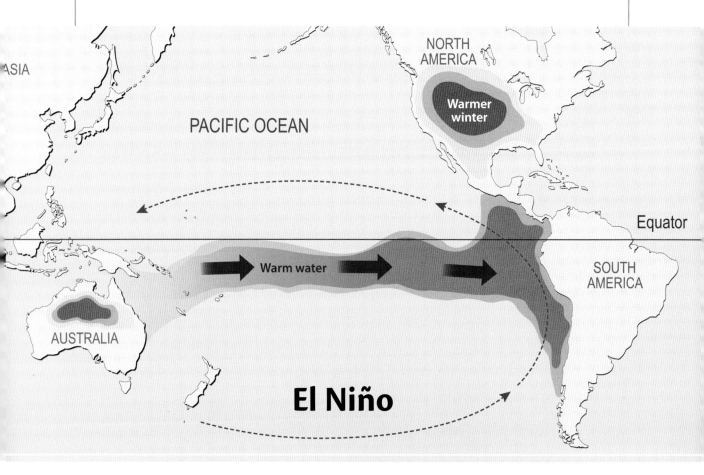

Severe drought has damaged corn grown in the midwestern United States.

During El Niño, warmer waters also cause the Pacific **jet stream** to move farther south. Parts of the northern United States and Canada become drier and warmer. Areas of India, Australia, and Indonesia may have drought instead of their typical heavy rain. Parts of Japan and China may have heavy rain and floods.

Another climate pattern that impacts temperatures is La Niña. It also takes place every two to seven years, but it tends to happen less often than El Niño.

La Niña has the opposite effect of El Niño. During La Niña, east winds are stronger than usual. They push warm water toward Asia. Cold water rises to the surface along the western coasts of North and South America. The southern United States may have drought. The Pacific Northwest and Canada may have heavy rain and floods.

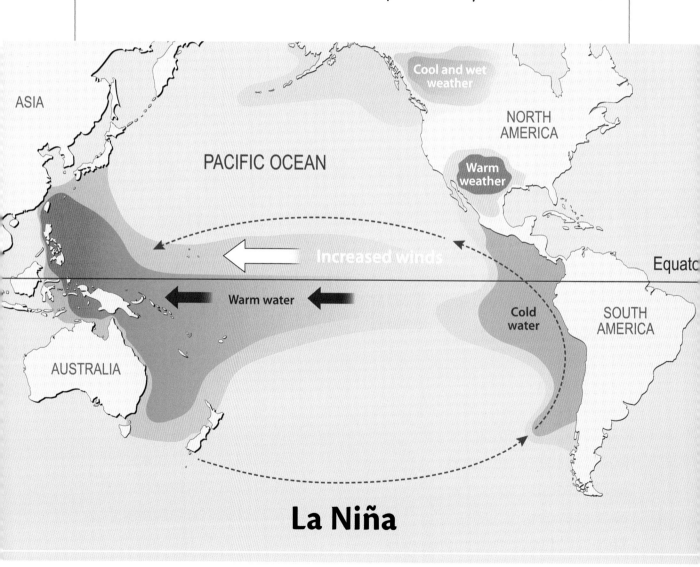

La Niña

Flooded city streets in Bangladesh as a result of heavy rains during the summer of 2023

Although El Niño and La Niña have short-term impacts on climate, many scientists think human-driven climate change can affect these climate patterns. As the planet gets warmer from greenhouse gas emissions, temperatures during El Niño and La Niña will shift. El Niño years will become hotter and hotter. La Niña years will also warm up, lessening the usual cooling effect. El Niño and La Niña will happen more often as well. During these times, there will be heavier rainfall in some places and less in others. Weather patterns will become unpredictable. This could make life harder for many living things.

Global Impacts

Global temperatures are often cooler during La Niña and hotter during El Niño. In the past several years, the El Niño and La Niña patterns have been very irregular. The record heat of 2023 marked the end of a three-year La Niña. At the same time, a strong El Niño season started. This brought higher temperatures that lasted for several months. Changing El Niño and La Niña patterns are one reason Earth is experiencing extreme heat waves.

A street thermometer in Sevilla, Spain, shows the scorching temperature of 50°C (122°F).

FACT

In Spanish, "El Niño" means "little boy." "La Niña" means "little girl." The names were given by South American fishermen. They were the first to notice these climate patterns.

DEMONSTRATING THE GREENHOUSE EFFECT

Understand the greenhouse effect by doing this simple science experiment.

WHAT YOU NEED

4 glass jars
plastic wrap
4 large rubber bands
white vinegar
baking soda
meat thermometer

WHAT YOU DO

1. Cover the opening of one empty jar with plastic wrap. Wrap a rubber band around the plastic wrap to seal the jar tight.

2. Add ¼ cup of vinegar to the second jar. Seal it with plastic wrap and a rubber band.

3. Add one tablespoon of baking soda to the third jar. Seal it with plastic wrap and a rubber band.

4. Add ¼ cup of vinegar and one tablespoon of baking soda to the fourth jar. Seal it with plastic wrap and a rubber band.

5. Place all four jars near a sunny window for 30 minutes.

6. One at a time, use the meat thermometer to poke a small hole in the plastic wrap of each jar. Measure the temperature inside each one. Which jar has the highest temperature?

WHAT HAPPENED?

The fourth jar should have the highest temperature because the baking soda and vinegar react to make carbon dioxide. As the jar sits in the sun, the trapped gas makes the jar hotter, just like greenhouse gases make Earth's atmosphere warmer.

CHAPTER 2

THE EFFECTS OF RISING TEMPERATURES

Earth's rising temperatures have major impacts around the globe. As Earth warms faster than normal, weather patterns become unpredictable. Storms and floods happen more often. They also become more intense. Warming ocean waters lead to more cyclones, typhoons, and hurricanes.

Warming temperatures also melt polar ice and **glaciers** faster. As they melt, more freshwater is added to the oceans. The added freshwater makes saltwater less dense, which causes ocean currents to cool and slow down. This makes it hard for some marine animals to survive. In addition, melting polar ice and glaciers cause sea levels to rise. Over time, coastal towns may suffer from flooding and **erosion**. Humans and animals may lose their homes.

Warmer winter temperatures can also reduce snowfall. This is a problem because snow reflects light. With less snow on the ground, Earth absorbs more light and surface temperatures increase. In addition, some animals, such as salmon, rely on icy snowmelt to survive. Less snowfall means less snowmelt flows into streams where salmon live. At the same time, rising surface temperatures heat the streams. A combination of lower water levels and warmer water temperatures makes it difficult for salmon to survive.

FACT

Melting glaciers can also lead to more volcanic eruptions. As glaciers melt, less pressure weighs down on Earth's surface and more liquid magma forms in Earth's mantle. Over time, these changes can fuel volcanic eruptions.

Enormous chunks of ice breaking off the Hubbard Glacier in Alaska

Meanwhile, rising temperatures and changing rainfall patterns cause problems for farmers. Too little rainfall can cause crops to wither in fields. Too much can cause crops to rot or wash them away completely. In some cases, long periods of little to no rainfall lead to terrible droughts. In 2023, even the Amazon Rainforest suffered from drought. Many villages lost access to water as rivers dried up.

Along with drier weather come wildfires. These fires destroy everything on land and **pollute** the air. They also force people and animals from their homes. In 2023, many countries, including Greece, Spain, Canada, and Portugal, suffered from major wildfires. The fires were fueled by warmer and drier weather.

A devastating wildfire raging in northern Greece in 2023

Heat Wave Timeline

1936: **NORTH AMERICA HEAT WAVE**
Temperatures passed 90°F (32°C) in the Midwest for more than 10 days. Crops were destroyed, and many people died from the heat.

1987: **GREECE HEAT WAVE**
For one week, temperatures reached 104°F (40°C). Many lives were lost.

1995: **CHICAGO HEAT WAVE**
Summer temperatures reached 106°F (41°C). Power was lost, transportation stopped, and many lives were lost.

2010: **EASTERN EUROPE HEAT WAVE**
Summer temperatures reached 100°F (38°C) in parts of Russia. Crops were destroyed, and wildfires raged. Many people died.

2015: **INDIA HEAT WAVE**
Temperatures skyrocketed to 117°F (47°C) in some parts of India. Many lives were lost.

2022: **CHINA HEAT WAVE**
About 70 days of intense summer heat, with some areas reaching 104°F (40°C). The heat cost many people their lives.

2022: **NORTH AMERICA HEAT WAVE**
California, Arizona, and Nevada experienced record-breaking temperatures as high as 116°F (47°C). Many lost their lives.

2023: **UNITED STATES, CHINA, AND SOUTHERN EUROPE HEAT WAVES**
Heat records were broken, and wildfires were a major threat. People around the world lost their lives.

What the Future Holds

The planet needs our help. People need to change their behavior to reduce Earth's rising temperatures. If good changes don't happen soon, the rising temperatures will impact the future.

Right now, Earth is losing **species** 1,000 times faster than at any time in recorded human history. If the planet keeps getting hotter, scientists worry that one million species may become extinct within a few decades. In addition, two-thirds of the planet's glaciers will disappear by 2100. This massive melting will disrupt water systems that plants and animals need to survive.

Warmer weather also allows mosquitoes, ticks, and other insects to multiply. These insects can carry diseases that make some people and animals sick. On top of that, warm temperatures may cause some animals to leave their natural **habitats** and move closer to people. These uncommon contacts with people could spread diseases more easily.

A zookeeper releases a koala back into its habitat after it was affected by the 2020 wildfires in Australia.

With temperatures rising and extreme weather becoming more common, many people may need to move as well. They may need to find safer places to live with more access to food and water.

The Maui Wildfire

Homes and businesses destroyed by the 2023 wildfire in Lahaina, Hawaii

In 2023, a deadly wildfire struck the island of Maui, Hawaii. Residents were shocked. Many people thought that a tropical island was safe from wildfires. But climate change made one happen. The island had recently experienced a drought. A mix of high temperatures, strong winds, and low humidity caused the fire to burn fast and far.

CHAPTER 3

WORKING TOGETHER FOR CHANGE

Earth's temperatures may be rising, but there's still some good news. Many people and organizations are working hard to cool down the planet. In 2015, 196 countries signed a **treaty** called the Paris Agreement. They agreed to reduce greenhouse gas emissions in their countries to slow climate change. Their goal is to limit Earth's warming temperature by 2.7°F (1.5°C) by 2100.

Since the treaty was signed, many countries have made progress. Here are just some of the actions taken across the globe:

- The United States is creating some electricity with little to no carbon emissions. Wind energy, solar energy, and technology that limits the release of carbon dioxide are all being used. Tax credits are also being offered to households that use solar panels for energy.

- Zimbabwe has adopted a green jobs program. It aims to create more farming jobs.

- Printing companies in North Macedonia and Finland are using solar energy to power their printing machines.

- Chile is constructing environmentally friendly buildings and using low-carbon transportation.

- Papua New Guinea has improved its logging practices to reduce the negative impact of deforestation.

- Somalia has built dams that help people and animals access clean water, especially during droughts.

While these actions are a great start, more work is needed to slow the rise in Earth's temperature. World leaders will need to continue to work hard to meet their climate goals.

Fortunately, governments aren't working alone. Many companies are reducing their greenhouse gas emissions—and helping their customers do the same. Some companies use solar energy and reduce waste. Others use reusable or recyclable packaging. Clothing companies are even finding ways to use recycled materials to make new clothes. And some food companies produce plant-based meat substitutes to reduce methane emissions from raising cattle.

A shopper compares two plant-based meat substitutes at a grocery store.

Some companies also make products that use cleaner energy sources. This helps reduce greenhouse gas emissions. For example, some car companies sell electric vehicles. These cars do not burn fuel, so they don't release greenhouse gases. Instead, they get their power from rechargeable electric batteries. While making and charging these batteries releases some emissions, electric cars release less emissions overall than gas-powered cars.

Appliance companies also sell products that use less energy. New refrigerators, washing machines, and dishwashers all have energy-saving technology. They use the smallest amount of energy possible to run.

An electric car at a charging station

Young Activists for Climate Change

Some young people are working hard to slow climate change. Greta Thunberg has led protests around the world and spoken at many conferences. Autumn Peltier fights for clean water for Indigenous people. Lesein Mutunkei started Trees4Goals. He encourages soccer players to plant trees for every goal they score. Jerome Foster II started a youth activist group called OneMillionOfUs. He is the youngest person to serve as an adviser for the White House.

Autumn Peltier

FACT

Many companies make their products using environmentally friendly processes. Samsung and LG make some electronics from recycled plastic. Mattel makes some toys from sugarcane and other plants. Patagonia produces clothing made from recycled plastic bottles.

CHAPTER 4

HOW YOU CAN HELP THE PLANET

Helping the planet starts with each person taking small steps. And some of these steps you can do at home. For instance, you can turn off devices and lights when not in use. You can replace old light bulbs with energy-saving LED bulbs. Also try adjusting the temperature on your home's thermostat to use less heat and air conditioning. You can even encourage your family to install solar panels on your home or in your yard. These panels capture and turn sunlight into electricity. All of these things can help reduce the creation of greenhouse gases by lowering the demand for electricity.

Another way to help the environment is to encourage your family and friends to reuse and recycle materials. Buying used appliances and furniture reduces the need for metal and wood. Buying used toys and clothes reduces the need for plastics and fabrics. You can also use less plastic by avoiding **disposable** water bottles, cups, straws, plates, and utensils. All of these items use energy and create waste when they are made. By using reusable items instead, you can help reduce the demand for more disposable items.

People can do a lot to reduce greenhouse gases in their communities as well. One small step is to use environmentally friendly transportation when possible. Walking, biking, and using kick scooters are good for your body and the environment. Driving electric or **hybrid** cars reduces the creation of carbon dioxide. Many cities also have buses and trains that use renewable energy sources.

Whole communities work together to save energy and reduce waste too. Yard sales encourage people to buy used items. Recycling and **composting** bins can be placed around a city and inside public buildings such as hospitals. Restaurants and grocery stores can find ways to donate unused food. Park and beach cleanups can bring communities together. Environmental clubs can spread knowledge about important issues and help keep schools clean too.

While there is a lot we can do to help the planet, it's also important to speak up when more changes are needed. If a community is not doing enough to help the environment, talk to local representatives or the mayor. If you have an idea for a way to help the environment, ask people to sign a petition. Adding more voices to a special cause can bring about good changes.

Ultimately, it will take people working together around the world to keep Earth from reaching a boiling point. The future is ours to make.

BUILD A BOTTLE GARDEN

This garden can help the environment in two ways—by recycling and keeping the air clean!

WHAT YOU NEED

3 2-liter plastic bottles
scissors
large nail
long piece of twine
potting soil
vegetable or flower seeds

WHAT YOU DO

1. Lay a 2-liter plastic bottle on its side.

2. Use the scissors to cut a large rectangle out of one side of the bottle. Be sure to leave a plastic edge around the rectangle—do not cut out the entire side of the bottle.

3. Use a large nail to punch two holes in the bottle. Each hole should be near a short side of the rectangle.

4. Turn the bottle over. Punch two more holes in the bottle. These holes should align with the holes made in step 3.

5. Repeat steps 1 through 4 with the other two bottles.

6. Thread one half of a long piece of twine through the punched holes on one end of a bottle. Thread the other end of the twine through the punched holes on the other end of the bottle. Tie knots under the bottom holes of the bottle to keep it in place on the twine.

7. Continue threading the remaining lengths of twine that are hanging beneath the first bottle through the remaining two bottles. Distance the bottles evenly before tying them in place.

8. Hang the bottles in a sunny spot on an outside wall, fence, window, or balcony.

9. Fill the bottles with potting soil and plant some seeds in each one.

10. Water your bottle garden and watch it grow.

GLOSSARY

atmosphere (AT-muhss-fihr)—the mixture of gases that surrounds Earth

bacteria (bak-TEER-ee-uh)—single-celled microscopic creatures that exist everywhere in nature

carbohydrate (kar-boh-HYE-drate)—a substance found in foods such as bread, rice, cereal, and potatoes that gives you energy

climate change (KLY-muht CHAYNJ)—a significant change in Earth's climate over a period of time

composting (KAHM-poh-sting)—a natural process of recycling organic matter into a fertilizer to enrich soil and plants

decompose (dee-kum-POZ)—to break down into smaller parts through a chemical process

deforestation (dee-for-ist-AY-shuhn)—the removal of trees

disposable (dis-POH-zuh-buhl)—able or meant to be thrown away

drought (DROUT)—a long period of weather with little or no rainfall

emissions (ee-MI-shuhnz)—substances, such as gases, released into the air

equator (ee-KWAY-tuhr)—an imaginary line that divides the northern and southern hemispheres of Earth

erosion (ee-ROH-zhuhn)—the wearing away of land by water or wind

glacier (GLAY-sher)—a large mass of flattened snow and ice

greenhouse gases (GREEN-houss GASS-ez)—gases in a planet's atmosphere that trap heat energy from the sun

habitat (HAH-bih-tat)—an environment where plants and animals naturally live

hybrid (HI-brid)—a mix of two different types; hybrid engines run on electricity and gasoline or diesel fuel

jet stream (JET STREEM)—a fast-flowing air current high in the atmosphere

pollute (puh-LOOT)—to make something dirty or unsafe

species (SPEE-sheez)—a group of similar living things that can reproduce

treaty (TREE-tee)—an agreement put in writing

READ MORE

Golkar, Golriz. *Ancient Ice: What Glaciers Reveal About Climate Change.* North Mankato, MN: Capstone Press, 2024.

Jaycox, Jaclyn. *Wildfire, Inside the Inferno.* North Mankato, MN: Capstone Editions, 2023.

Perdew, Laura. *Your Sustainable World: A Kid's Guide to Everyday Choices That Help the Planet!* North Mankato, MN: Capstone Press, 2025.

INTERNET SITES

Center for Climate and Energy Solutions: Climate Basics for Kids
c2es.org/content/climate-basics-for-kids

Climate Kids: A Guide to Climate Change for Kids
climatekids.nasa.gov/kids-guide-to-climate-change

Nemours KidsHealth: Be a Green Kid
kidshealth.org/en/kids/go-green.html

INDEX

ABOUT THE AUTHOR

Golriz Golkar has written more than 100 books for children. Inspired by her work as an elementary school teacher, she loves to write the kinds of books that children are excited to read. Golriz holds a B.A. in American literature and culture from UCLA and an Ed.M. in language and literacy from the Harvard Graduate School of Education. She loves to travel and study languages. Golriz lives in France with her family. She thinks children are the very best teachers, and she loves reading and learning with her young daughter every day.